MARK MY WORDS:

A COLLECTION OF MY LIFETIME POEM

DR. HO CHEE KIT

INDIA · SINGAPORE · MALAYSIA

ISBN 979-8-89133-934-7

Contents

ACKNOWLEDGEMENT

Many thanks to the people I know
Showing love to such a tiny minnow
It's like sunlight coming through the window
Until I couldn't even see my shadow

PREFACE

These poems are my life reflection
Read them to regulate your emotion
These poems are my original collection
Keep them to educate your generation

AUTHOR'S BIOGRAPHY

He is Dr. Ho Chee Kit
He exercises to keep himself fit
He is not a popular hit
He just does his best bit

He enjoys cooling under the sun
He prefers walking to just run
He enjoys writing poem for fun
He prefers adding humour and pun

5

Life we make it paramount

Let's ensure a good account

Love we give right amount

Let's ensure every moment count

Never bother sleeping a wink
Seeing your face turn pink
When the health index sink
You'll realize the hidden link

Some have really good upbringing
Enduring pain that keeps coming
Some neglect their own feeling
Enduring agony without achieving anything

6

Life has a side called ugly
Who would discover the hidden beauty
See the reason behind life's misery
Enlightenment will be more than likely

Pondering through a troubled sleepless night
Forgetting those episodes of inevitable fight
Exploring true ideas you willingly might
Assuring those outcomes that's absolutely right

There's no syllabus for life's decision

Trial and error sometimes bring tension

Keep track of your life's mission

And always keep your inner passion

First collect all the good memories

Then write your own creative stories

When in doubt clear the worries

You're the answers to your queries

Transform into the wind of night

Immerse into the wonder of sight

Looking into the radiance of light

Reaching into the mountain of height

7

We went through enjoyable time and ride

My arms are always by your side

We went through turbulent storm and tide

My arms are always ever open wide

The lake reflected the beautiful night sky
The ripples put my thoughts into lullaby
The nightingale sings as if to cry
The trees empathize but sadly cannot reply

My thoughts flow through like no other
The wind blows me a little shiver
My thoughts flow through like a river
The mind blows away my pain forever

People pleasers you better be a slave
Otherwise give your bosses what they crave
People forgivers you better be very brave
Otherwise bring your regrets to the grave

If the pain hurts very much so

Be prepared to quickly let it go

If the love not very much so

Be prepared to quickly let her go

Great to see each other hand hold
Better than each other busy collect gold
Great to see each other grow old
Better than each other separate early fold

Love it simple and love it strong
Love it sincerely you'll never go wrong
Let me play you this wonderful song
Let you be touched and sing along

Make our life mission loud and clear

Don't just listen we must also hear

Overcome challenges we cry a happy tear

May our world survive many more light-year

Human life can be full of beauty
But it's hard to keep it bounty
So do cherish every moment with dignity
Never mind if it's not a reality

To get a brochure search the counter

To get the fella search the hammer

To borrow money avoid a local banker

To borrow time avoid a restless lawyer

The road ahead hasn't been usually bright
Walking through together in a lantern light
The skyline carved out a beautiful night
Bringing back the long gone joyful sight

Getting ourselves entangled in a love triangle

We burn both sides of a candle

Getting into a quarrel nobody can handle

We soon put ourselves in deep trouble

Wonderful things appear to catch our attention
Great things start with a simple notion
Not everyone will listen to your suggestion
Let them continue with their life's education

As the frog jumps over the drain

That is when it begins to rain

As the fog covers your thinking brain

That is when it reveals its pain

Always at the top of your game

Need courage and determination all the same

Fail there's no one else to blame

Enjoy success because the breakthrough finally came

As we go through autumn and summer
Our hearts go through sorrow and laughter
Someone said life is a roller coaster
It's difficult to put two people together

Don't attach to anybody like a glue

Check out yourself for the right clue

Don't bother seeing the sky dark blue

Check out the fact false or true

You can talk until the cow moo

You can jog until the cat poo

You can talk until the crowd boo

You can jog until the rest too

8

We continue to accumulate our wealth through addition
Greedily growing our money and estate through multiplication
We distribute to our left-behind beneficiaries through division
Readily realizing our best life lived through subtraction

Choose to buy people the food they crave
Never bring your wallet in order to save
Choose to forgive people you can be brave
Never bring along your regrets to the grave

Sitting inside a train fighting fever and cold
Looking outside the window wrapping arms and unfold
Sitting inside the office growing lonely and old
Looking outside the window reflecting stories that's untold

Prepare well today for a better movie cast
Live healthy today for a life long last
Prepare well today for a time passing fast
Live fullest today for a better future past

When you're young you like to run around
Bringing joy to everyone who hear your sound
As you grow older you gain some pound
The hair on top your head rarely found

Frequently exercising the brain we feed new memories
Throwing away the doubts we clear the worries
Writing down the answers we satisfy our queries
Clearing away the hurdles we create amazing stories

Staring into the night sky at the balcony

Absorbing the dark energy and the abundant mystery

Pondering the movement of the infinite heavenly body

Wondering how will they determine our own destiny

In a world full of agony and fantasy

We can't let ourselves go hungry or thirsty

At the cafeteria order coffee tea not brandy

Go back to work without any more worry

The road ahead may be a bit jittery

But be honest in your pursuit of glory

When people doubt you show them the contrary

Complete the journey and write your success story

Worry not that you're not in the pack

Worry about what good attributes you actually lack

When you fail don't hide inside a sack

Come out and show you'll make a comeback

Warm weather can consider diving into a pool
Wearing a mask should make you look cool
Working adults can consider going back to school
Wise men should stop arguing with a fool

The pain of tripping down a single stair
Reminds me of calming down on a chair
The pain of accumulating grief going into despair
Reminds me of capturing sorrow in the air

Vehicles on the road home are standing still
The massive traffic jam has gotten you ill
Before you start thinking about your anxiety pill
Take a deep breath as you always will

Showering you love from young to youthful teen

Your aging parents keep asking where you've been

Let them know that you are still keen

Before their images disappear forever no longer seen

Strangers can sometimes make our face go wry
Friends often make us want to quickly deny
We have motivational speakers to make people cry
And the right strategies to make you buy

Getting in touch with a dangerous love potion
It's like setting yourself for a paralyzed condition
How cruel it can invoke a deepest emotion
Suffering through your life on a long-term medication

I want to fill my life with content

I don't want or need your every consent

I want to chill my life with content

I don't want or need your every comment

9

The joy of walking splashing water through the stream
Reminds me of myself to never forget the cream
The joy of shouting venting frustration through the scream
Reminds me of myself to never forget the dream

You ask me why after today we expect tomorrow

The same reason why after lending then we borrow

You ask me why after happiness we expect sorrow

The same reason why after spring then summer follow

A bishop may not be better than a knight

What happened in the day can happen at night

A peaceful compromise may be better than a fight

What we initially thought wrong can be proven right

Wearing a spectacle may not make you an uncle

Watching a turtle may not make you a bicycle

Observing yourself forever change going through the life cycle

Keeping yourself forever young will definitely be a miracle

Let your life play out collection of beautiful song
Sharing with everyone the music where love always belong
Let your warmth sparkle the righteous not the wrong
Spreading around the globe like the wind blowing strong

Eating raw seaweed can make you want to vomit

Doing something stupid can make you an instant hit

High cholesterol level these people need to stay fit

Wise leaders their advice people better think about it

Dying without getting old makes us all feel pitiful

Overcoming life's obstacles teaches us how to be grateful

Spending time with your loved ones we feel wonderful

Growing wrinkles and grey hair together makes life beautiful

People try to get away from life's pulsating pace

Searching diligently for a getaway to a breathtaking place

Some people live so long competing in amazing race

Wondering if they would rather die with amazing grace

Laugh at me I just ignore the initial source

Focus on me I just complete the entire course

Obstacle upon me I just find more alternate resource

Happy for me I just feel proud of course

10

As you grow old your eyes become snowy and blurry
Your weak leg and body sometimes need people to carry
As you grow old your tongue can't take anymore curry
Your weak digestive system sometimes makes you even more hungry

In many bakeries we can buy fragrant bun and cake

In many relationships we can decide to destroy or make

In many stories we can know what's true and fake

In many relationships we can decide to give or take

Traveling around the world in game of fix and patch
We are all waiting for the right egg to hatch
Traveling around the world in game of chase and catch
We are all waiting for the right soul to match

We won't have to worry about flood due to monsoon

When you can afford to never wake up before noon

We won't have to worry about celebrating Raya too soon

When you can see only the stars before the moon

Keep your pace nobody can tease you for being slow
Just make sure you think deep through your bone marrow
Then your decision will be as sharp as an arrow
The path it travels will be the one to follow

The land below the skies captured our pursuit of glory

The graveyard beneath the ocean revealed our degree of morality

The days between the nights created our chronicles of history

The life before the demise realized our forces of mortality

No drink you cannot bring; no song without the singling

No fame without the shame; no post without the mailing

No complain you cannot explain; no pain without the tingling

No grain without the rain; no love without the tenderling

Breathing the last breath meeting again in a soft lullaby
It feels sad to have no tears to even cry
Breathing the lost faith meeting again in a distant nearby
It feels comforting to have no reason to ask why

To enjoy the summer, drink cold water as you shower
To cross the river, take off your shoe and sweater
To enjoy the laughter, share a joke with your sister
To cross the thunder, prepare to walk a little slower

Laugh your way to dexterity, eat cherry and drink brandy

Love a life with purity, kiss mommy and hug daddy

Lead your will to divinity, hide fallacy and seek trinity

Live a life with priority, forgive affinity and forget infinity

Growing our wrinkles and grey hair makes life so beautiful
Dying our hair without getting old makes us feel pitiful
Overcoming our life's obstacles teaches us how to be grateful
Spending our time with our loved ones we feel wonderful

Get out look beyond and don't let your past stay

Whatever you have done there is a price to pay

Get out look beyond and don't let your friends pray

Whatever you have done there is a consequence some day

Nobody cares about you being born with a silver spoon
When you can't differentiate between the sun and the moon
Nobody cares about you sleeping late waking up at noon
When you can't sense that you are arriving too soon

11

95

Having a severe toothache is a result of too much sweet

Having a warm heart is better than having some cold feet

Having a bad record is a result of too much tweet

Having a good dialogue is better than going to the street

Expressing real joy could be better than showing fake animated condolence

Battling high emotions could be better than cycling through vicious recurrence

Standing solidly firm could be better than trying to show indifference

Staying quietly humble could be better than trying to parade confidence

Don't put the blame on the floor if you can't dance

Do something no one has done before if you can't enhance

Don't put the blame on the door if you can't glance

Do something no one has done before if you can't advance

12

A day when you feel love after you put on a blanket

A day when you feel warm after you put on a jacket

A day when you buy my book after it's in the market

A day when you build my legacy after I kick the bucket